GARDEN MATH

KATIE MARSICO

Lerner Publications ◆ Minneapolis

To Nico Filice—one of the bravest boys I know

Lerner Publications Company
A division of Lerner Publishing Group, Inc.
241 First Avenue North
Minneapolis, MN 55401 USA

For reading levels and more information, look up this title at www.lernerbooks.com.

Photo Acknowledgments
The images in this book are used with the permission of: © WJBurgwal/iStock/Thinkstock, p. 1 (sunflower); © iStockphoto.com/rusm, p. 1 (graph paper); © Richard Clark/Getty Images, p. 4; © Laura Westlund/Independent Picture Service, pp. 5 (flower bed), 11 (pumpkins), 21 (growth chart); © Bozena_Fulawka/Collection/Thinkstock, p. 5 (tomatoes); © Image Source//Getty Images, p. 6; © iStockphoto.com/spxChrome, pp. 7, 9, 11, 12, 13, 17, 23, 27 (notebook); © iStockphoto.com/Diane Lobambarbe, p. 7 (strawberries); © Jack Hollingsworth/Getty Images, p. 8; © brozova/iStock/Thinkstock, p. 9 (pansies); © Gabe Palmer/Alamy, p. 10; © Simone Capozzi/iStock/Thinkstock, p. 12 (tape measure); © iStockphoto.com/alubalish, pp. 13, 21, 27 (torn paper); © threeart/iStock/Thinkstock, p. 13 (pumpkin); © Ariel Skelley/Blend Images/Getty Images, p. 14; © iStockphoto.com/dimitris66, p. 15 (daisies); © iStockphoto.com/timsa, p. 15 (marigolds); © Fuse/Getty Images, p. 16; © iStockphoto.com/Chris_Elwell, p. 17 (watering can); © Westend61/Getty Images, p. 18; © iStockphoto.com/Lauri Patterson, p. 19 (lima beans); © TongRo Images/Alamy, p. 20; © iStockphoto.com/venturecx, p. 21 (kale field); © altrendo images/Getty Images, p. 23; © Aleksy Fursov/Hemera/Thinkstock, p. 23 (roses); © John Howard/Getty Images, p. 24; © iStockphoto.com/WestLight, p. 25 (darker eggshells); © iStockphoto.com/rrocio, p. 25 (lighter eggshells); © Patrick Molnar/Getty Images, p. 26; © bajinda/iStock/Thinkstock, p. 27 (watermelon); © yanikap/iStock/Thinkstock, p. 28; © GregorBister/iStock/Thinkstock, p. 29.

Front cover: © yobro10/iStock/Thinkstock (girl), © iStockphoto.com/rusm (graph paper).
Back cover: © iStockphoto.com/photka.

Main body text set in Conduit ITC Std 14/18. Typeface provided by International Typeface Corp.

Library of Congress Cataloging-in-Publication Data

Marsico, Katie, 1980- author
      Garden math / by Katie Marsico.
         page   cm — (Math everywhere!)
      Audience: Ages 8–10.
      Audience: K to grade 3.
      ISBN: 978-1-4677-1887-5 (lib. : alk. paper)
      ISBN: 978-1-4677-8630-0 (pbk. : alk. paper)
      ISBN: 978-1-4677-8631-7 (EB pdf)
      1. Mathematics—Juvenile literature. 2. Gardening—Mathematics—Juvenile literature. 3. Word problems (Mathematics)—Juvenile literature. I. Title.
   QA141.3.M344 2016
   513—dc23   2014038832

Manufactured in the United States of America
1 — CG — 7/15/15

TABLE OF CONTENTS

Tomato Totals..4

Build a Bed 6

Parallel Petunias 8

Make a Pumpkin Prediction!............................ 10

A Square Compromise 14

Ready for a Refill 16

What's Best for the Beans? 18

Plan to Plant! 20

Raising Roses 22

Figure out the Formula! 24

Moneymaking Melons 26

Ready, Set, Grow!..28

Answer Key... 30
Glossary.. 32
Further Information.. 32
Index 32

TOMATO TOTALS

What a lovely day to stroll through the garden! But be sure to bring a calculator! Gardens are filled with beautiful flowers, nutritious foods, and math. Without math, people would have a hard time growing and harvesting plants. Want to know more? Roll up your sleeves and start digging!

Gino and Grandpa are planting a tomato garden in a raised, rectangular bed. It measures 10 feet (3 meters) long by 4 feet (1.2 m) wide. Grandpa explains that it's important not to overcrowd the tomatoes. Otherwise, they won't have enough room to grow properly.

The seedlings need to be spaced about 2 feet (0.6 m) apart. The rows will run lengthwise, and Gino and Grandpa need to leave 3 feet (0.9 m) between each row.

The width of the bed ÷ the distance needed between rows = the number of spaces between rows that will fit in the garden.

If there is room for, say, three spaces between rows, four rows will fit in the garden.

The length of the bed ÷ the distance needed between plants = the number of plants that will fit in each row. The diagram shows an example of these distances.

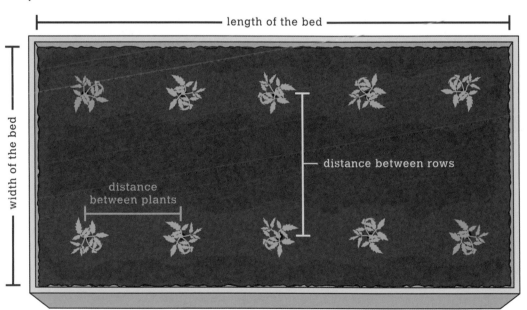

length of the bed

width of the bed

distance between rows

distance between plants

How many rows of tomato plants will fit in the raised bed? How many plants will Grandpa and Gino be able to grow?

Check your answers to all math problems on pages 30—31.

BUILD A BED

Waste not, want not! That's what Meg and her aunt think. Meg and Aunt Jen plan to grow 12 strawberry plants. First, though, they need to build a raised wooden bed.

Meg suggests buying wood at the hardware store. But Aunt Jen has a better idea. She just took apart her backyard deck. There's plenty of wood left over that would be perfect for their strawberry bed. Each plank measures 8 feet (2.4 m) long, 8 inches (20 centimeters) wide, and 2 inches (5.1 cm) tall.

Aunt Jen says she'll take care of sawing the wood. In return, Meg promises to help her tackle any math that the project requires.

Meg was hoping to make their strawberry bed look like the one at the local greenhouse. So when she was there a few weeks ago, she took measurements. The bed at the greenhouse is 8 inches (20 cm) tall and 3 feet (91 cm) wide. Each board in that bed stands on its skinny 2-inch (5.1 cm) side.

Unfortunately, Meg forgot to measure its length. It's after 5 p.m. and the greenhouse is closed, so she can't go back and check. Still, Meg thinks she'll be able to figure it out. She knows that the 12 strawberry plants shouldn't be spaced less than 12 inches (30 cm) apart. Meg also knows that **12 inches = 1 foot (30 cm).**

First, Meg plans to figure out how long the raised bed needs to be to fit all 12 plants. Then she needs to find the perimeter of the bed.
Perimeter = the sum of the lengths of all the sides. How long should the strawberry bed be? How many of Aunt Jen's planks will they use to build it?

PARALLEL PETUNIAS

People often say that school is a place to grow. So what better spot for flowers? Luke and Bess ask Principal James if the student council can plant a school garden. He agrees and offers to clear a space in front of the building. It will measure 6 feet (1.8 m) long and 4 feet (1.2 m) wide. In this case, the width is the distance from the back of the garden to the front of the garden. Principal James thinks it would be cool for the garden to feature the school colors—purple and white.

Luke and Bess agree. Fortunately, the garden center down the street is having a petunia sale. Luke and Bess find many different kinds of petunias. They buy their four favorite types. Two are purple, and two are white.

The next day, Luke and Bess sketch a few possible blueprints, or design plans. Bess wants to plant in parallel rows. Parallel lines run side by side, like railroad tracks. They never intersect, or cross. Luke loves Bess's idea. He suggests switching colors between rows: purple, white, purple, white, and so on.

Does it matter which color row they start with? Absolutely! Taller plants should go toward the back of the garden. That way, sunlight will reach all the plants. Bess and Luke already know that the back row of their garden will be white. One of the white petunias they chose grows about 15 inches (38 cm) tall. The other three varieties should reach a height of only 10 inches (25 cm). None of their petunias should be spaced closer than 8 inches (20 cm) apart.

What color will the front row of the school garden be?

MAKE A PUMPKIN PREDICTION!

Halloween's almost here! So it's nearly time for the Giant Jack-o'-Lantern contest. In Lin's town, local farmers compete to produce the biggest pumpkin. This year, Lin is volunteering at Smith Farm. Each week, she helps Mr. Smith track the growth of his two biggest pumpkins.

Of course, it's not easy to weigh huge fruit. So Mr. Smith and Lin rely on three other measurements to estimate weight. One is the pumpkin's circumference. That's the distance around the edge of a circle. Mr. Smith and Lin figure out circumference with a cloth tape measure. They stretch it horizontally around the pumpkin's widest point. Then they measure the distance in inches. Large pumpkins tend to grow on their sides, so the stem will be on the side of the pumpkin.

Next, Mr. Smith and Lin take two "over-the-top" measurements. For the first, Lin holds one end of the tape measure on the ground, alongside the stem and perpendicular to the ground. Mr. Smith records how far it stretches over the pumpkin's top and back to the ground on the opposite side. They do almost the same thing for their second "over-the-top" measurement. The only difference is that the last measurement is perpendicular to the first "over-the-top" measurement.

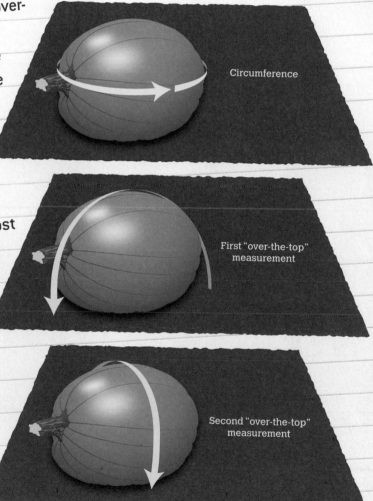

Circumference

First "over-the-top" measurement

Second "over-the-top" measurement

Mr. Smith and Lin add all three measurements together and round to the nearest 5 inches (12.7 cm). Then they search for this rounded sum in the table. The number to the right of it is the pumpkin's estimated weight. In most cases, estimates are within 10 percent, or 0.10, of a pumpkin's actual weight.

Inches (cm)	Estimated pounds (kg)
165 (419)	105 (48)
170 (432)	114 (52)
175 (445)	124 (56)
180 (457)	134 (61)
185 (470)	144 (65)
190 (483)	155 (70)
195 (495)	167 (76)
200 (508)	179 (81)
205 (521)	192 (87)
210 (533)	205 (93)
215 (546)	219 (99)
220 (559)	234 (106)
225 (572)	249 (113)
230 (584)	265 (120)
235 (597)	282 (128)
240 (610)	300 (136)

The harvest at Smith Farm is just a few days away. Mr. Smith and Lin prepare to make their final estimates. Pumpkin A has a circumference of 98 inches (2.5 m). Its over-the-top measurements are 58 inches (1.5 m) and 54 inches (1.4 m). The circumference of pumpkin B is 95 inches (2.4 m). Its over-the-top measurements are 62 inches (1.6 m) and 65 inches (1.7 m).

Based on the weight estimates in the chart, which pumpkin is more likely to be a winner? Should Lin be surprised if either pumpkin ends up weighing 10 pounds (4.5 kg) less than she estimated? How about 20 pounds (9.1 kg) less?

DO THE MATH!

You're visiting a pumpkin farm in late summer. The farmer says you've come at a peak growing time. During August, his giant pumpkins gain about 30 pounds (14 kg) a day! He tells you he just measured the biggest one. Its circumference is 75 inches (1.9 m), and its two over-the-top measurements are 48 inches (1.2 m) and 44 inches (1.1 m). Estimate the pumpkin's weight. If today is August 20, how heavy do you predict the pumpkin will be by September 1?

A SQUARE COMPROMISE

Marigolds! No, daisies! No, marigolds! No, daisies! Ralph and his sister, Eva, don't see eye to eye about gardening. Today they're arguing about what to plant. Ralph likes marigolds, but Eva prefers daisies. They just can't agree on what to grow!

Luckily, Mom tells them they don't have to. Yesterday she cleared a square patch of yard for them to work in. It measures 5 feet (1.5 m) long by 5 feet wide. Mom surrounded the perimeter of the patch with a folding garden fence. She'll simply use more fencing to divide that space into two equal parts.

One option is to split the patch into two rectangles. Another is to put 7.1 feet (2.2 m) of fence between two opposite diagonal corners. If Mom does this, the square patch will become two triangles. Eva and Ralph's math teacher would call the dividing fence the line of symmetry, since the parts on each side match.

Either way, Ralph and Eva hope to plant around the perimeters of their gardens. **A rectangle's perimeter = the sum of the lengths of its sides.** The same formula is used to calculate a triangle's perimeter.

Ralph knows that his marigold seeds should be spaced 1 inch (2.5 cm) apart. Eva needs to keep 2 inches (5.1 cm) of space between her daisy seeds. **How many seeds will each of them be able to plant around the perimeter of a rectangular garden? How about a triangular garden? Which option will let each of them plant more seeds?**

READY FOR A REFILL

Normally, Kayla loves sunny skies. This week, however, she wishes she'd see more rain clouds. Kayla agreed to water her neighbors' garden while they're on vacation. But over the weekend, the hose she was using sprung a leak. It's completely useless!

At first, Kayla wasn't too worried about the flowers. The weather forecast called for rain. But the forecaster was wrong. For three days, it's been sunny! The forecaster is predicting the dry spell will last another week. Kayla knows her neighbors won't be home for five more days. So she finally grabs a watering can from her garage.

She also phones a nearby greenhouse. Kayla wants to know exactly how much water to use. Earlier, she was just spraying the hose for a few minutes. Working with a watering can requires more math skill.

Kayla estimates that the garden measures about 3 feet (91 cm) long by 3 feet wide. She also knows that her neighbors are growing a kind of plant called annuals. The clerk at the greenhouse says that the dryness of the ground has to be considered too. He concludes that the garden needs about 5 gallons of water a day.

Kayla stares at her watering can. The label on the bottom says it holds 1.5 liters. Kayla does some research and learns that

1 gallon = 3.8 liters.

How many times will she need to fill the watering can today? If the dry spell lasts until her neighbors return, how many times will she need to fill the can in total?

(Round up to the nearest full can.)

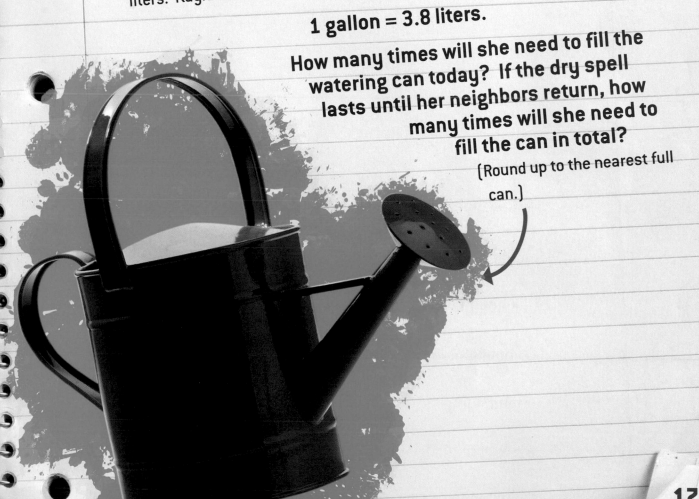

WHAT'S BEST FOR THE BEANS?

Sonya and Tom are trying to learn how water affects the growth of lima beans. Sonya and Tom plant 18 beans. They divide the pots into three equal groups: groups A, B, and C. Every day, Sonya and Tom use a dropper to give the plants in group A 5 milliliters (0.17 fluid ounces) of water. The plants in group B get 7 milliliters (0.24 fl. oz.). The beans in group C receive 10 milliliters (0.34 fl. oz.) of water. At the end of two weeks, Sonya and Tom measure the height of each bean plant. They record their data in the following table:

Growth of Individual Bean Plants

Group	Plant	Heights in inches (cm)
A	1	2.7 (6.9)
A	2	2.9 (7.4)
A	3	3.1 (7.9)
A	4	2.8 (7.1)
A	5	3 (7.6)
A	6	3.1 (7.9)
B	7	4.9 (12.4)
B	8	5 (12.7)
B	9	4.9 (12.4)
B	10	5.2 (13.2)
B	11	5.1 (13)
B	12	5 (12.7)
C	13	3.9 (9.9)
C	14	3.4 (8.6)
C	15	3.6 (9.1)
C	16	3.5 (8.9)
C	17	3.5 (8.9)
C	18	3.4 (8.6)

Whew! Tom and Sonya sure have a lot of numbers to crunch! They also have to figure out a way to present their findings to their class. Neither of them thinks reading a list of 24 numbers is a good idea. Their classmates will fall asleep!

Sonya has a better suggestion. She says they should calculate the average growth for each group of bean plants.

Average growth = the sum of the heights of the plants in a group ÷ the number of plants in that group.

Sonya and Tom decide to create a second table. (See below.) **What numbers should go in the final column? Which group of plants grew the most? What amount of daily water helps lima beans grow best?**

Average Bean Plant Growth by Group

Plant group	Daily water amount in milliliters (fl. oz.)	Average plant growth
A	5 (0.17)	
B	7 (0.24)	
C	10 (0.34)	

PLAN TO PLANT!

Avi's rabbit, Max, enjoys a diet of fresh kale and carrot and radish tops. The veterinarian says mustard and collard greens are also good for Avi's pet. Avi's excited when Dad suggests growing their own bunny food. First, though, they need to plan a growing schedule. The ground will be too cold to plant anything until early spring.

Dad says a table will help them keep track of important dates. So Avi gets a pencil, paper, and their calendar. Dad researches when they should plant and harvest. Climate and location affect how vegetables grow. Certain plants develop best during certain date ranges. And not all vegetables need the same amount of growing time, either.

Avi will plant his seeds on March 25. Once he knows the average growing time for his vegetables, he can estimate when to harvest them. **What dates should Avi add to the last column of his table?** (Use a calendar if you need to.)

Vegetable	Average growing time	Recommended planting dates	Possible harvest dates
radishes	25–30 days	March 25 to May 1	
mustard greens	40–50 days	March 25 to May 1	
kale	50–70 days	March 25 to April 5	
collard greens	55–70 days	March 20 to April 10	
carrots	70–80 days	March 25 to April 10	

DO THE MATH!

Suppose you're planting mustard greens and kale for your pet guinea pig. Ideally, your harvest dates will be *at least* a week apart. You'd prefer to harvest the mustard greens first. You plant them on March 25. **What's the earliest you should plant the kale?** Use Avi's chart to figure out your schedule! Play it safe and use the latest possible harvest date for the mustard greens. Use the shortest possible growing period for the kale.

RAISING ROSES

Welcome home! Ruth and her family just moved into their new house. Ruth notices a card taped to the back door.

We left you a housewarming gift. Near the back gate, you will find nine rosebushes. We left half a bag of fertilizer in the shed to help you take care of them.

—Bloom family (previous owners)

Ruth knows that fertilizer helps plants grow and stay healthy. And that's exactly what she wants for her beautiful new rosebushes. Each is bursting with delicate pink, yellow, white, or red buds.

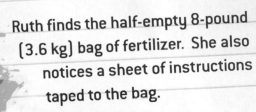

Ruth finds the half-empty 8-pound (3.6 kg) bag of fertilizer. She also notices a sheet of instructions taped to the bag.

Use ¾ cup (113 grams), or about 0.25 pounds, per bush every six weeks from March through October. So far, we have fertilized once—on March 5. Good luck!

Ruth makes a table to help her figure out when to fertilize. It's March 7 today. **How many more times should Ruth add fertilizer to the rosebushes? When will she have to buy a new bag?**

Ruth's Fertilization Cheat Sheet		
Fertilization date	**Amount of fertilizer used**	**Amount of fertilizer left**
March 5		½ bag

FIGURE OUT THE FORMULA!

Wait! Don't throw out that old banana peel! Trey needs it for his homemade fertilizer. He's also using eggshells, Epsom salt, and water. Trey is following his grandma's secret formula. He's confident it must work, since he's seen her gorgeous garden. Trey is less sure how to prepare the secret mixture, though. It's not that Grandma won't share her formula. In fact, she recently mailed Trey a handwritten copy of it.

Trey, if you follow the directions below, you'll end up with about 129 grams (4.6 oz.) of dry powder. This is the formula:

eight parts dried banana peel (about four peels)

one part dried eggshell

one part Epsom salt

Your parents should help you blend the banana peels and the eggshells in a food processor. Next, stir in the Epsom salt. Then add your secret powder to a 32-ounce (946 ml) spray bottle. Fill the bottle with water and shake well. Spray the fertilizer on soil and watch your plants bloom!

Grandma wrote down how many dried banana peels to use. It looks as if she also noted amounts for the eggshells and Epsom salt. Unfortunately, Trey can't read those two numbers because the ink on the card she sent smudged. So he needs to figure out what "*one part* dried eggshell" and "*one part* Epsom salt" mean.

Luckily, his mom has an idea. First, she explains that when Grandma says "parts," she means percentages. Together, the dried banana peels, eggshells, and Epsom salt form 10 parts, or 100 percent, of the powder. So the eggshells should make up 10 percent, or 0.10, of the weight of the finished powder. Next, Mom uses her food scale to weigh a single dry eggshell. It weighs about 5.1 grams (0.2 oz.). Banana peels make up eight parts, or 80 percent, of the total. Knowing that, **how many eggshells should Trey use? How many grams of Epsom salt?** Round to the nearest whole eggshell and gram.

MONEYMAKING MELONS

It takes money to make money, even in a garden. Sam and Jon's Uncle Tim owns a fruit stand at the local farmers' market. So Uncle Tim offers them a business opportunity. He asks Sam and Jon if they'd be interested in growing ruby watermelons for his fruit stand.

He wants to price the melons at 35¢ per pound. A fully grown ruby watermelon is usually 6 to 8 pounds (2.7 to 3.6 kg). Uncle Tim says he'll give Sam and Jon 90 percent of whatever he earns by selling their fruit. He'll even provide most of their gardening supplies. Sam and Jon would be responsible for buying enough seeds for a single harvest. They'd also have to pay for two garden rakes.

Uncle Tim offers the kids a patch on his farm to grow 32 groups of watermelon seeds. He recommends planting three seeds per group. Eventually, Sam and Jon should trim away two of the plants and leave only the best one in each group. This improves the odds of raising strong, healthy watermelons.

After talking to Uncle Tim, Sam and Jon head to the garden center. They hope to get a rough idea of their expenses. A packet of 10 watermelon seeds costs $5.95, and garden rakes are $9.97 each. As Sam and Jon leave, they notice a sign by the checkout lanes. It mentions a 6.25 percent sales tax.

How much will Sam and Jon spend if they accept Uncle Tim's offer? Assuming all their watermelons grow and weigh between 6 pounds and 8 pounds (2.7 to 3.6 kg), what's the most they might earn? Will it be more or less than their expenses?

DO THE MATH!

Looking to buy insects to keep your garden healthy? Ladybugs devour aphids and other pests that eat plants. You compare prices at three companies. The first advertises 1 pint, or 4,500 ladybugs, for $29.98. Shipping costs are already included. The second company offers 300 ladybugs for $3.50. Shipping and handling are $5.25. Finally, for $14.42, you can pick up ½ pint of ladybugs at the local hardware store. Which company offers the cheapest ladybugs?

READY, SET, GROW!

Ready to grow some plants? Before you put your green thumb to the test, you have a few final math problems to tackle. Then you can plan your own garden!

The director of the local community center has decided to build a butterfly garden. This weekend, you've volunteered to help. The space you'll use measures 10 feet (3 m) long by 12 feet (3.7 m) wide. Yet the director plans to divide the land into four smaller plots—plots A, B, C, and D. Each one will be the same size but will have a different combination of flowers that appeal to butterflies.

The director has 24 garden stakes. She asks you to divide the land in half by placing a line of stakes lengthwise across the space. She makes another line going across the width, dividing it in half the other way. You know from math class that **the perimeter of a plot = the sum of the length of its sides.**

What is the perimeter of each of the smaller plots?

Next, you start planting sunflower seeds in plot A. The director suggests arranging them in rows that run along the width of the plot. You will need about 3 feet (9.1 m) of space between each row. The sunflowers should be planted in groups of two or three seeds spaced about 2 inches (5.1 cm) apart. **How many sunflower seeds will you plant in plot A?**

Today is April 3. The seed packet says it takes sunflowers two to three months to fully develop. **When should you expect them to bloom and begin attracting butterflies?**

Answer Key

Page 5 Two rows of tomato plants will fit. (4 ft. ÷ 3 ft. between rows = 1.3, or about one space separating 2 rows)
They can grow 12 tomato plants. (10 ft. ÷ 2 ft. between plants = 5 spaces between plants/row, or 6 plants /row; 6 plants/row × 2 rows = 12 plants)

Page 7 The strawberry bed should be at least 2 feet (61 cm) long. (3 ft. × 12 in. = 36 in.; 36 in. ÷ 12 in. between plants = 3 spaces; 3 spaces allows for 4 plants per row; 12 plants ÷ 4 plants/row = 3 rows; 3 rows need two 12 in. spaces between rows; 2 × 12 in. of space = 24 in.; 24 in. ÷ 12 in./1 ft. = 2 ft.)
They will need 1¼ planks of Aunt Jen's wood. (2 ft. [length] + 2 ft. + 3 ft. [width] + 3 ft. = 10 ft.; 10 ft. ÷ 8 ft. [plank length] = 1.25 planks, or 1¼ planks)

Page 9 The front row will be white. (4 ft. × 12 in./1 ft. = 48 in.; 48 in. ÷ 8 in. between plants = 6 spaces between rows; 6 spaces allows for 7 rows; back row = row 1 = white; row 2 = purple; row 3 = white; row 4 = purple; row 5 = white; row 6 = purple; row 7 = white = front row)

Page 13 Pumpkin B is more likely to be a winner. (Pumpkin A: 98 in. + 58 in. + 54 in. = 210 in.; a 210 in. pumpkin is about 205 lb. Pumpkin B: 95 in. + 62 in. + 65 in. = 222 in.; a 222 in. pumpkin is about 240 lb.; 240 lb. > 205 lb.)
Either pumpkin may end up being 10 to 20 pounds (4.5 to 9.1 kg) lighter than she estimated. (205 lb. × 0.10 = 20.5 lb.; 240 lb. × 0.10 = 24 lb.)

Do the Math!
The pumpkin's estimated weight is 109 pounds (49 kg). (75 in. + 48 in. + 44 in. = 167 in.; 167 in. is about 109 lb.)
The pumpkin will probably weigh 469 pounds (213 kg) by September 1. (Aug. 20 − Sept. 1 = 12 days; 12 days × 30 lb./day = 360 lb.; 360 lb. + 109 lb. = 469 lb.)

Page 15 Ralph could plant 181 marigold seeds in a rectangular garden. Eva could plant 91 daisy seeds. (½ × 5 ft. = 2.5 ft.; 2.5 ft. + 2.5 ft. + 5 ft. + 5 ft. = 15 ft. [perimeter]; 15 ft. × 12 in./1 ft. = 180 in.; 180 in. ÷ 1 in. between marigold seeds = 180 spaces, or 181 marigold seeds; 180 in. ÷ 2 in. between daisy seeds = 90 spaces, or 91 daisy seeds)
Ralph could plant 206 marigold seeds in a triangular garden. Eva could plant 103 daisy seeds. (5 ft. + 5 ft. + 7.1 ft. = 17.1 ft. [perimeter]); (17.1 ft. × 12 in./1 ft. = 205.2 in.; 205 in. ÷ 1 in. between marigold seeds = 205 spaces, or 206 marigold seeds; 205 in. ÷ 2 in. between daisy seeds = 102.5 spaces, or 103 daisy seeds)
Two triangular gardens will let them plant more seeds.

Page 17 Kayla will need to fill the watering can 13 times today. (3.8 L/gal. × 5 gal. = 19 L; 19 L ÷ 1.5 L/can = 12.7 cans, or about 13 cans)
She will need to fill it 65 times if the dry spell lasts until her neighbors return. (13 cans/day × 5 days = 65 cans)

Page 19 The average growth for group A is 2.9 inches (7.4 cm). (2.7 in. + 2.9 in. + 3.1 in. + 2.8 in. + 3 in. + 3.1 in. = 17.6 in.; 17.6 in. ÷ 6 plants = 2.9 in.) The average growth for group B is 5 inches (12.7 cm). (4.9 in. + 5 in. + 4.9 in. + 5.2 in. + 5.1 in. + 5 in. = 30.1 in.; 30.1 in. ÷ 6 plants = 5 in.) The average growth for group C is 3.6 inches (9.1 cm). (3.9 in. + 3.4 in. + 3.6 in. + 3.5 in. + 3.5 in. + 3.4 in. = 21.3 in.; 21.3 in. ÷ 6 plants = 3.6 in.) The plants in group B grew the most, so 7 milliliters (0.24 fl. oz.) of water a day seems to help lima beans grow best. (5 in. > 2.9 in.; 5 in. > 3.6 in.)

Page 21 Avi should add these dates to his chart: radishes, April 19–24; mustard greens, May 4–14; kale, May 14–June 3; collard greens, May 19–June 3; and carrots, June 3–13.
(Radishes: Mar. 25 + 25 days = Apr. 19; Mar. 25 + 30 days = Apr. 24; mustard greens: Mar. 25 + 40 days = May 4;

Mar. 25 + 50 days = May 14; kale: Mar. 25 + 50 days = May 14; Mar. 25 + 70 days = June 3; collard greens: Mar. 25 + 55 days = May 19; Mar. 25 + 70 days = June 3; carrots: Mar. 25 + 70 days = June 3; Mar. 25 + 80 days = June 13]

Do the Math!
The earliest you should plant the kale is April 1.
[Mar. 25 + 50 days = May 14 + 7 days = May 21; May 21 − 50 days = Apr. 1]

Page 23

Fertilization date	Amount of fertilizer used	Amount of fertilizer left
March 5	2.25 lb. (1 kg)	4 lb. (1.8 kg)
April 16	2.25 lb.	1.75 lb. (0.8 kg)
May 28	2.25 lb.	7.5 lb. (3.4 kg)
July 9	2.25 lb.	5.25 lb. (2.4 kg)
August 20	2.25 lb.	3 lb. (1.4 kg)
October 1	2.25 lb.	0.75 lb. (0.3 kg)

Ruth should fertilize five more times, on April 16, May 28, July 9, August 20, and October 1. [Mar. 5 + 6 wks. = Apr. 16; Apr. 16 + 6 wks. = May 28; May 28 + 6 wks. = July 9; July 9 + 6 wks. = Aug. 20; Aug. 20 + 6 wks. = Oct. 1]
She'll need more fertilizer after April 16 and after October 1. [8 lb./bag × ½ bag left = 4 lb.; 0.25 lb./bush × 9 bushes = 2.25 lb.; 4 lb. − 2.25 lb. = 1.75 lb.; 1.75 lb. < 2.25 lb. needed for the next treatment on May 28; 1.75 lb. left + 8 lb. in the new bag = 9.75 lb.; 9.75 lb. − 2.25 lb. = 7.5 lb.; 7.5 lb. − 2.25 lb. = 5.25 lb.; 5.25 lb. − 2.25 lb. = 3 lb.; 3 lb. − 2.25 lb. = 0.75 lb.; 0.75 lb. < 2.25 lb. needed for the next treatment in Mar.]

Page 25 Trey should use three eggshells. [129 g of powder × 0.10 = 12.9 g of eggshells needed; 12.9 g ÷ 5.1 g/eggshell = 2.5 eggshells, or about 3 eggshells]
He should use 12.9 grams (0.5 ounces) of Epsom salt. [129 g of powder × 0.10 = 12.9 g Epsom salt]

Page 27 Sam and Jon would spend $84.41. [32 groups × 3 seeds/group = 96 seeds; 96 seeds ÷ 10 seeds/packet = 9.6 packets, or about 10 packets; 10 packets of seeds × $5.95/packet = $59.50; 2 rakes × $9.97/rake = $19.94; $59.50 + $19.94 = $79.44; $79.44 × 0.0625 sales tax = $4.97; $79.44 + $4.97 = $84.41]
The most they might earn is $80.64. [32 plants × 8 lb./plant = 256 lb.; 256 lb. × 0.35/lb. = $89.60; $89.60 × .90 = $80.64]
Their potential earnings are less than their expenses. [$80.64 < $84.41]

Do the Math!
Company 3 offers the cheapest bugs. The price per ladybug, about 0.6¢, is less than company 2's price of about 3¢ per ladybug and less than company 1's price of about 0.7¢ per ladybug. [Company 1: $29.98 ÷ 4,500 ladybugs = 0.007, or 0.7¢/ladybug. Company 2: $3.50 + $5.25 = $8.75; $8.75 ÷ 300 ladybugs = 0.029, or about 3¢/ladybug. Company 3: 4,500 ladybugs/pt. × ½ pt. = 2,250 ladybugs; $14.42 ÷ 2,250 ladybugs = 0.006, or 0.6¢/ladybug; 0.6¢/ladybug < 0.7¢/ladybug; 0.6¢/ladybug < 3¢/ladybug]

Page 29 **Ready, Set, Grow!**
The perimeter of each smaller plot is 22 feet (6.7 m). [10 ft. × ½ = 5 ft.; 12 ft. × ½ = 6 ft.; 5 ft. + 5 ft. + 6 ft. + 6 ft. = 22 ft.]
You will plant 148 to 222 sunflower seeds in plot A. [5 ft. ÷ 3 ft. = 1.7 spaces, or enough room for a 3 ft. space between 2 rows; 6 ft./row × 12 in./1 ft. = 72 in./row; 72 in. ÷ 2 in. between groups = 36 spaces between groups, or 37 groups; 37 groups × 2 seeds/group = 74 seeds; 37 groups × 3 seeds/group = 111 seeds; 74 seeds × 2 rows = 148 seeds; 111 seeds × 2 rows = 222 seeds]
Your sunflowers should bloom between June 3 and July 3. [Apr. 3 + 2 mos. = June 3; Apr. 3 + 3 mos. = July 3]

Glossary

annual: a plant that usually lives for only one growing season

average: the sum of a group of numbers divided by the size of that group

circumference: the length of the edge around a circle

estimate: to calculate without using exact numbers or information

harvest: to gather crops or other plants that have been raised for food

parallel: staying the same distance from each other and never crossing

perimeter: the distance around the edge of a shape or a space

perpendicular: at right angles to a surface or a line

Further Information

Cornell, Kari. *The Nitty-Gritty Gardening Book: Fun Projects for All Seasons.* Minneapolis: Millbrook Press, 2015. Dig into these gardening projects for step-by-step instructions on how to grow plants at home.

Kids Gardening
http://www.kidsgardening.org
Check out this site for gardening ideas, information about starting a garden at your school, and even recipes for your harvest.

Kids Growing Strong: Butterfly Gardens
http://kidsgrowingstrong.org/butterfly-gardens
Get more information on how to design and plant a butterfly garden.

Perritano, John. *Pools to Ponds: Area, Perimeter, and Capacity.* Chicago: Norwood House Press, 2013. Find out more about methods of measurement that are useful in everyday situations.

Index

average, 19

circumference, 11, 13

diagrams, 5
distance, 5, 8, 11
division, 14–15, 28–29

estimating, 11–13

fertilizing, 22–23, 24–25

garden beds and plots, 4–5, 6–7, 8–9, 14–15, 27, 28–29

gardening expenses, 27
growing schedule, 20–21, 29

harvesting, 21
height, 9, 18–19

length, 5, 7, 8, 14, 17, 28
line of symmetry, 15

measuring and measurements, 6–7, 11–13, 17, 18–19, 23

parallel lines, 9
percentages, 25

perimeter, 7, 14–15, 29
plant growth, 10–13
predicting, 10–13

sales tax, 27
shipping costs, 27
spacing, 5, 7, 9, 15, 29

tables, 12, 19, 21, 23

watering plants, 16–17, 18–19
weight, 11–13, 25, 26–27
width, 5, 7, 8, 14, 17, 28